The Diary of a Stay-At-Home Mom

The Diary of a Stay-At-Home Mom

Savage Encounters

Marilyn Black

To order additional copies of this book, contact:
Xlibris
844-714-8691
www.Xlibris.com
Orders@Xlibris.com
830360

Contents

Acknowledgments

This book would have never been published without the encouragement and support of my friends and family.

Alexzander, thank you for pushing me to publish my own work as I tried to convince you to publish yours. YOU'RE NEXT! Get crackin', kid!

Mom, thank you for always being so supportive of my writing. Although I still think you are biased!

Michael, my love, thank you for supporting me as I pursued publication! You've had my heart from day one and kept me sane during the chaos.

Jessica, my bestie! Thank you for being my friend when I felt all was lost.

My lovey, thank you for being a shining light in the darkness . . . I will never forget you, Tracey.

There are so many more people that I could probably fill a whole other book with them! Even random strangers on the game World of Warcraft, people I had never met in person, and those who would indulge me in haiku battles, role-playing, or improve poetry!

Never forget: The only one setting limits is yourself, and you'll never know if you can if you don't try.

Everybody is a genius. But if you judge a fish by its ability to climb a tree, it will live its whole life believing that it is stupid.
—Unknown

Being Positive doesn't mean you walk around with rose-colored glasses. It means you overcome the thorns.
—John Gordon and Daniel Decker

Whatever you do, work at it with all your heart, as working for the Lord, not for human masters.
—Colossians 3:23

What I thought was beyond impossible . . . actually came true . . . I know, with all my heart, it can be the same for you.
—Christine Canales

Add

Sitting in the classroom, looking at the board . . .
It's math again; oh, help me, dear Lord . . .

Numbers and lines blurring into a mess.
Jumbled and confused; *"how is my answer less?"*

"Move this over here, but only when I say!"
"See now, for this one, you move it <u>this</u> way."

Now we're in science and I understand some.
But formulas and triangles . . . man, I feel dumb.

I can't keep them straight! There's so many, you see . . .
Why can't I get it? I think it's just me.

Oh great, now history, I'm out, I just quit.
All these dates and names, not one can I get.

I'm stupid, I'm dumb, I'll never understand.
They just don't get it . . . even a C would be grand.

Why try? I'll just fail and even my teachers agree.
Just leave me alone with my music; just please . . . leave me be.

Delving into books, my only escape.
A hero, a dragon, a vampire with a cape!

These are much better than the reality I face.
Years go by, confidence gone . . . leaving not a trace.

Kid to teenager, teenager to adult.
Self-worth worn to nothing, leaving scarcely a bolt.

Then a teacher I once knew saw me in a parking lot.
She worked for a company and said they had a spot!

I applied on a fluke, not really expecting anything.
A call actually came! The phone really did ring!

Later, I was accepted, and at work I did my best!
But the training to be had put coworker's patience to the test.

At first I was discouraged and felt stupid again . . .
But found different ways of learning; it got easier! And then . . .

Life happened, I had to quit but later felt a pull.
"Go back to college," it said, but I was stubborn as a bull.

"I'LL FAIL AGAIN!" I screamed as I tried to run away.
Life had other plans, and I would defiantly pray.

Ultimately, the answer was "GO," and I was scared to death.
I walked into those doors, not knowing I held my breath.

If I said those years were easy, that would be a lie.
Sometimes, I got so frustrated, I would break down and cry.

But graduation day came . . .
My mentality was never the same.

While a student, I did my best; asked questions, unafraid to impose.
Hands shaking, I asked another to pin honors' tassels to my robe.

I didn't fall, I didn't even trip!
My heart, however, did do a little skip.

What I thought was beyond impossible ... actually came true ...
I know, with all my heart, it can be the same for you

A penguin doesn't wish it could fly like the doves.
Instead, it happily swims and eats the fish that it loves.

I'll be frank, not everything is possible, you may hit a wall.
A wall so wide and tall, you may never succeed at all ...

You can't sprout new legs, nor grow a new brain.
Sometimes, there are concepts you just can't retain.

Does that mean you are worthless or dumb?
No, sweet one, you think there are none, but trust me, you have some!

Some talent or skill you have yet to find!
Believe me, you have a truly brilliant mind!

The problem is, it's shackled, you see ...
It can't show its skill, all it can be!

Buried in muck as dark as the night.
You have to be willing to dig it out, to put up a fight!

So push out those thoughts of "I can't."
Find a NEW saying to chant!

My heart breaks for you, I wish I could "fix it."
Climb into your brain and patch any broken bit.

Toss out the negative and polish all the good.
Take down all the cobwebs before closing up the hood.

Leaving nary a stone unturned, nor dark corner unobserved.
If only I could do that, teach the lesson that I learned.

Alas, all I can do is encourage, love, and do my best.
Give you all the "tools" in my belt for your quest.

I believe in you, I know you can do this!
If you never try, who knows what you'll miss!

Potential unending and talented, it's true!
The only one setting up those limits . . . is you.

—Christine Canales

Disclaimer and Warning

DISCLAIMER: Calling my children as natives and savages, I am not referring to Native Americans or Indians.

Rather, I am referencing the placement of any "missionary" into an uncivilized and uncultured land. Not meaning dumb or caveman people but rather a people that know no rules and have no limits.

The phrasing "native" and "savage" simply mean as they are. In this storyline, I am an alien, unknown to these parts. They, however, are native—born into it.

No heritages or people were harmed, mimicked, or belittled in the making of these diaries.

WARNING!
My experiences and definitions in this diary will not mirror yours. Should you decide to venture into this territory as I have, your experience may be better or worse than my own.

Week 1

Today, I embark on the toughest job in the world. I will be entering a savage country. I am no longer working in order to provide an income for a village. There is no telling what awaits me in this unknown land. I can only hope that it is easier than my previous visits have been. I have a local native to work with, but he is doing as I was previously and utilizing his skills to bring a meager income to our land. He is essential to sustaining life!

However, this will be the first time I will have delved headlong into a territory dominated by three lone savages. I have worked with them in the past and the oldest native has become familiar with the English language, but the other two tiny natives still speak in only grunts and screams.

I don't know if my purpose here will be for long. I can only hope and pray that I can civilize these natives and show them a better world, a higher knowledge, and the kindness my own missionary showed me when I was a native and she was the alien visiting savage lands.

These diaries will be kept to mark progress and to show others that these conditions can be survived in. Perhaps one day, I will look back and laugh at any misfortune . . . in the meantime . . . keep this lone traveler in your prayers . . . .

—Mom

Week 2

If anyone is reading this . . . please send reinforcements! There is no semblance of order, no common language, and no rules! A complete free-for-all and the toughest challenger wins!

This is far more difficult than I anticipated. The first order of operations will be: to find common ground and create some sort of routine. Hopefully, this will placate the upheaval of my new arrival and my sanity can return!

I have a long road ahead of me, but I believe that perseverance and tough love will get me through.

Please keep me in your thoughts! I fear that my strength will leave me if I truly believe that I am alone in this . . . .

—Mom

Week 3

Well, it's week three in savage territory. For some reason, the locals seem to think that I am their only source of entertainment. I had to do cleaning, and we didn't go outside for the first time since I landed on this unfamiliar soil.
They. Went. Insane.

It seems that sunlight and exhausting activity appease them. I shall make note of this for future cleaning days.

For now, I have left them with an adult local and retreated to the kitchen to cook. Perhaps food will take the edge off their screaming demands.

As for tomorrow, I have plans for a thing called "the li-br-ary." This tactic has worked before. I will utilize it.

—Mom

Week 4

It's week four in savage territory.

The rules here are skewed. It appears rough play is only acceptable if administered by the oldest native. Any other less-than-gentle play is unacceptable to him, even by the other locals.

Food here is plentiful, but the consumption of it is low. Strange. They don't seem to need fuel to be as hyper as a squirrel on caffeine.

No rest is allowed. The locals seem to think naptime is a cruel torture mechanism. I must break them of this. Books seem to help.

The locals don't seem to understand that certain things cause them pain. I must develop a better system and monitor the situation vigilantly. Until next time, I hope we can all stay alive!

—Mom

Week 4 and 5 Days

The tiny natives either think that I have a weight problem, or seem to think that I don't require food to function.

Last night, they flooded me with "more" and "food" as soon as I sat down with my pasta.

This morning, I made eggs, then gave them cereal and even some goldfish in an attempt to satisfy their hunger. I proceeded to make MY breakfast, a meager meal of bread and cream cheese. I left the room for two seconds and in come the little savages, each with a piece of bread in their hand and cream cheese smeared on hands, faces, and even a foot.

This could be a problem. I must find a way to communicate my distress.

P.S. The biggest savage finds it entertaining to rip things out of the wall. This must be broken . . . SOON.

Until next time, let's pray that my house is still standing.

—Mom

Week 5

Well, here I am again. It appears that the natives do not understand the concept of privacy or personal space. I have locked myself in the restroom in an attempt to urinate in peace. Their tortured cries and pitiful whimpers lead me to believe that they are near death.

This will not trick me again.

It is a lure to have the door be opened, so they can flood in and monitor my progress as well as disrupt the room by stringing toilet paper in various directions and flinging bath toys in my face.

I will remain strong.

Luckily, the inconvenient phenomenon that is the human body does not last long, and I am able to rejoin the chaos and attempt control by shouting various orders or questions such as "Get those underwear off your head!," "What is in your mouth?," "Why was your sister crying?," and the like.

Note to self:
We have yet to find an effective method of reining in the oldest savage. As he is the cause of most of the distress, a solution is imperative.

A wonderful thing called schooooool is coming soon. Perhaps education will civilize this rabidly hyperactive native.

I am now going to attempt to drink my beverage known as coffee. It is supposed to wake up and sharpen the mind. I have yet to benefit from this, but the flavor is savory.

—Mom

Week 6

It's week six in savage country.

I'm still alive. Today was cleaning day and it appears that this is unacceptable to the tiny natives. My work was constantly disrupted, and their screams of outrage echoed through our living quarters.

Sadly, a pet native called "Blue Dog" was down for the count. He received fatal wounds to his neck and tail while participating in "play." Our savages are none too gentle with our plushy friends and he was forced to be quarantined until first aid could be administered. Today, this has been accomplished. I am not a skilled surgeon, so the poor little blue dog is not the way he was. However, the gratitude of the savages has been immense in prior battle scenarios.

I am excited to present our repaired blue dog to the oldest native as a peace offering tomorrow. We shall see how it is received. Hopefully, he will view it as a miracle and be tame in body and mind as a result. I must keep my dreams alive!

—Mom

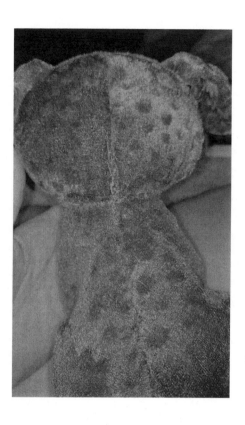

Week 7

We made it to another week, but something is strange today. It is awfully quiet in the village and one of the natives has gone MISSING!

Just kidding.

But it is still a strange feeling. The oldest native has come of age to attend prekindergarten, also known as pre-K. Things are much calmer than I anticipated. I am unsure of how to process this. Am I happy or sad? I'm going to decide on happy and try not to text his teacher to see how things are going.

I can only hope that my attempts at civilizing this tiny savage have taken root and he makes his village proud. Or reap havoc and leave chaos in his wake as he does at home. Let's hope it is not the latter.

—Mom

Week 7 and 5 Days

Greetings! The first week of attempting to civilize and educate the oldest native has been extremely tiresome. What are these new rules? I have been unable to locate such instructions and have had to use trial and error to verify acceptable procedures. However, I believe that I am learning the ropes of this confusing endeavor.

On another subject, having the tiny natives has always been a pleasure when their attitudes are placid. Recently, the lack of wrangling the oldest native has allowed me a bit more freedom, and I am able to better enjoy their silly antics. For example, my paltry attempts at educating these tiny natives have proven entertaining to say the least. Their unintelligible babble toward the ridiculous crayon characters on the television set has given me immense joy. Our progress on my attempt to teach colors is yet to be determined.

For the time being, I can understand the attraction to a job that can be so immensely frustrating and tiring.

Unfortunately, stress and frustration may be my constant companions, but I am happy to report that pure joy and satisfaction occur just as often.

—Mom

Week 8

Well, it's week eight in savage territory. I must confess that things have calmed down a bit. The tiny natives are learning my language of English, rather than the uncultured grunts and screams of the natives. I have succeeded in teaching them simple hand gestures or sign language when speech fails them.

This is a satisfactory approach as it lessens frustration for both parties.

Currently, the middle savage (whom I have taken the liberty of calling Jude, although he doesn't seem to understand the concept of the name just yet) has developed a favorite word: "Uh oh." Understandably, this causes confusion in the ranks. I must teach him that it is not an "uh-oh" if he purposefully launches a toy in his sister's direction. For obvious reasons, this is an unacceptable form of play.

This word also causes me distress when I am in the restroom and I hear a chorus of "Uh oh, uh oh!" after hearing the beep of the entertainment system being turned on.

On another note:

According to local legend, an awful occurrence called "the terrible twos" is well on its way. Facing this impending doom, I have but one request: Please pray for the sanity for all involved.

With loss of mind but not of life (yet), I bid you adieu, until next time.

—Mom

Week 9

This savage land has rapidly become the bane of my existence. A necessary evil, teeth are showing their ugly faces. The tiny natives seemed to be lacking several teeth and, at the time, I didn't think anything of it. However, it appears that these evil little things are breaking through gums and cause much discomfort and distress.

Cough cough. An illness has also swept into our tiny village. Rather than resting and sleeping these awful conditions off, the tiny natives respond in a baffling manner! Rising early, crying almost obsessively, and refusing to go any less than full throttle. Due to the excessive crying of the natives, lack of rest, and feeling unwell. I do believe that my demise will be soon. *Sneeze*

Do not cry for me, my friends. I am sure that the adult local native will avenge my death. Of course, this may be a bit dramatic, but I am willing to be prepared for every outcome. *Sniffle*

A holiday, the Day of Labor, has come upon us and therefore school is out of session. I do not refer to it as Labor Day but rather as "the Day of Labor," because today will be full of laborious events due to the extra "day off" as other countries so flippantly declare it. Regardless of my dismay, I will remember to whom this day was made for and thank our brave soldiers! I look forward to the day when this is once again a day of rest and reflection.

Should the overabundance of coughing, sneezing, and sniffling overtake my poor system . . . please know that I will not have died in vain. *Hand over heart.* I will remain true to my mission to the bitter end.

—Mom

Week 10

We survived the plague! The coughs and sniffles have gone down to a dull roar, and I am eternally grateful!

The natives seem to relish rising at ungodly hours, but beside the jubilant cries of the tiny natives, it has been relatively peaceful.

The gear required for transport can make one quite exhausted and everything becomes filthy. I took it upon myself to clean like a mad woman Saturday and the results have left me feeling fulfilled if not a bit tired. Of course, everything was immediately filthy once again in a couple hours. Can't say I didn't try! Our dependable vehicle for transportation has been shamefully neglected. Thankfully, the adult native assisted me in monitoring the tiny ones to prevent any disastrous occurrences during the cleansing.

Our means of transport no longer smells of old food, moldy sippy cups, and various household debris. You can imagine my feeling of accomplishment as this was a difficult feat and honestly rather disgusting. I will relish our next venture out of the household, gear and all.

On a side note:
It is that time of year for me to be inexplicably addicted to the art of "crochet," and once again, I have bitten off more than I

can chew by pursuing multiple projects that I have a feeling will never be completed . . . seeing as how I only know one official pattern . . . you can imagine my frustration with myself.

The first step is admitting that you have a problem . . . and there. I will leave you with bated breath, I'm sure. Until next time!

—Mom

Week 11

It is week eleven in this uncivilized land and I do believe that I am slowly becoming one of them. Childish songs plague my mind and unidentified food has become part of my wardrobe. I have begun to enjoy the ceaseless entertainment that is *Word World* and mimic the tiny native girl in her "YAH YAH" cries, which I assume to be her attempt in saying *Word World*.

My memory is fading from my clutches and my attention span is severely limited. Unfortunately, this is not out of the ordinary, which gives me a sense of doom regarding the teenage years of my pint-sized companions.

I fear that there is not much to report of the past week. Our little village is under strain from outside sources and therefore my attention has been drawn elsewhere. I will remain vigilant. I will conquer this strain and continue to civilize this land. The tiny natives are beginning to respond to simple commands such as "No," "Sit," "Clean up," and "Come here."

However, the tiny male native seems to extract much joy from running away from me as quickly as his little legs can possibly move, when he knows that he has an item in his clutches that I desire. This is less than satisfactory as it usually ends with him face down on the floor, mostly due to the lack of coordination. He looks like a panicked duck fleeing a scene. Suppressing my giggles has proven to be difficult, to say the least. Well, to err is human, after all.

I cannot wait to see what is in store this week.

—Mom

Week 12

My head is pounding, or perhaps that is the sound of the war drums the tiny natives have unearthed this past week. My adorable little natives have turned into heathens! I do not understand what switch was flipped, but someone PLEASE change it back!

The tiny natives have discovered the dreaded "mine" concept. I have no earthly idea how this is possible, as they cannot even articulate this yet! And the oldest native is no better! He has simultaneously decided that this week of all weeks was the perfect opportunity to revert back to his most uncivilized days: babyhood.

Not only are the tiny natives on a rampage, but all progress with the oldest seems to have flown the coop.

I am dreadfully tired, and while I adore my charges, I am more than ready for the next phase to approach quickly rather than slowly. Dear Lord, please grant me strength. I am unsure if my poor little brain can handle much more screaming.

Is there such a thing as screaming mother syndrome? Perhaps this is something that requires a diagnosis. Surely, a better name can be found; however, my poor head is reluctant to cooperate. In any case, I shall bid my adieu and wish you farewell.

—Mom

Week 14

The days are blurring; a week seems like a day and a day seems like a week. The incessant whining from the oldest native has become like a mosquito in my ear—unavoidable, inescapable, and the ever-present knowledge that it will draw the life out of me.

I apologize for missing the previous week. I acknowledge that no one may ever read these chronicles, but I must remain faithful. It is told that "One day, you will be able to look back on this and laugh." Well, I know this to be true, as I am laughing about events that have already passed. I look forward to the day where I can eat and utilize the restroom in peace, but until that day, I will be patient and vigilant.

This week's struggle has been with the mechanism known as the "back porch." The middle native seems to deem it necessary to test the strength of the said structure with his face. I fear that concrete is much sturdier than his chubby little cheeks. I must find a way to prevent these conflicts from occurring, before the local native services are contacted and I am reported for neglect or abuse of my charges.

Another problem that is surfacing is with the location of where the local canine defecates. The tiniest native thought it to be an ideal battle paint, which I strongly and emphatically disagree. I promptly washed it away, much to her delight in being able to splash in water. I previously had to remove the canine's source of water due to tiny natives using it as a birdbath. My progression with the outdoor play area is coming along nicely, and while they still trip and fall, it isn't nearly as often and I am not petrified of sticks or rocks impaling them.

The oldest native is attending school to further his civilization and learning. It has proven challenging to say the least, and the necessary evil that is "homework" is becoming a struggle; however, the benefits of developing good habits this early is imperative. I MUST stay strong!

I do not know when I will write again, but until then, keep me in your thoughts. Future self, if you are reading this, I hope all is well in your world and that all of these struggles have come to fruition.

Until next time,
Mom

Week 15

The days are still blurring; however, I have claimed victory with the canine fecal battle paint! I have discovered that daily removal of said feces prevents any bodily painting of any kind among the tiny natives.

With great dismay, I also realized that the disposal of my yard waste is not going to be as easy as I anticipated. It appears that stones, dirt, and trash are not allowed in my designated container. How absurd. I have resigned myself to separating the leaves/sticks, dirt, and stones into separate piles. The tiny natives make me believe that they will assist me, but once my back is turned, they scatter what they can with their tiny fists in all directions. I do believe this task will be inconvenient, to say the least, considering I have at least two more containers worth of leaves and sticks, along with two or more of dirt and considerable amount of stones to be rid of and only one said container. Keeping it all neat and separated will not be easy.

I apologize for dwelling on my simple chores, but as you can imagine, I am quite obsessed and eager to be done with this project.

My charges are a handful, but they are quite entertaining at times. Their lack of vocabulary and social graces makes them endearing, and I am eternally grateful to be blessed with them. These chronicles have become a source to vent frustration,

but I also realize that these little ones are pure treasures and irreplaceable. I look forward to the day when I see what kind of men and woman they become. It is impossible to tell right now, but I am eager to see how they grow and flourish.
I only pray that in the process, my sanity and patience remain intact.

Until next time,
Mom

Thoughtful Excerpt

Since becoming the sole provider of the tiny native's education and civilization, I have accepted the fact that any failure at all will directly implicate me as the source.

However, in studying these uncivilized beings in their natural habitat, I have become a bit envious of them. My attempts to civilize and introduce manners will in no way cease, but I have gained an appreciation for certain things.

For example, what is theirs is irrefutably theirs. They have no concept of loss or grief. Of course, until another native decides that the item is indeed not the original owners but in fact their own. But even then, the grief is short and they are easily placated with another shiny object.

Another is they depend wholly and completely on me. They have trust and peace beyond anything I have ever witnessed before. They know, without a shadow of a doubt, that food and shelter will be provided. They know that love is there and they have a rescuer, an "all-knowing" being that will undoubtedly provide their every need. Perhaps not their wants, but their needs to survive and thrive will be met.

I could go on forever, but this shall be my last point: They have no sense of pride or real greed. By this, I mean they are not compelled to perform tasks for the sake of their false pride or greed. Their greed only goes so far as a particular moment; they do not harbor jealousy at the display of another's wealth. They do not step all over beings lower than themselves to obtain a certain prize or level of achievement; rather, they want a thing and simply take it. Granted this is not always correct, but how simple a concept! They do not have wounded pride; they are just wounded at being disciplined. They are not greedy to a point of devoting their every day to grasp that something that they desire most.

Now, after saying all of this, I know one way or another they will no longer be savage and uncivilized after a time, regardless of the fact that I want them to be or not. Someone along the way will teach them things I don't want to be taught; this is why my mission is so vital. This is what drives me, why I strive to be better. I want them to be civilized adults, but I want them to have the fire that I have. The hope and peace I have found in God and my country. I have never wanted anything more than this, and failure has never seemed so close or as agonizing as it does with my charges.

One day, I will lose control of their environment. I can only pray and hope that any guidance I have to offer will outshine all the evil in this world. These chronicles may be a source of venting and my frustration now, but they will be my source of joy and remembrance in later years. I have written this excerpt to show my future self and any others that I do not belittle or think of my time with my charges as wasted effort, but rather as a beacon of hope to others, that their struggles and tribulations are not imagined, as well as show myself that I was never perfect or untouchable. These little humans have shown me what a pure heart really is, regardless of their infuriating actions and endless attempts to antagonize each other.

So, without further ado, I bid you farewell, until next time.

—Mom

Week . . . 16 or Whatever

My dear readers, I have fallen ill. A small matter considering the scheme of things, but inconvenient nonetheless. This illness has led me to sleep almost twelve hours, thanks to the constant vigil of the local adult native who cared for my charges while I was missing in action. However, this morning's events would have me believe that I hadn't slept at all!

The oldest native refused to listen or mind, which resulted in his immediate removal and placement into a corner. This delightful little technique is often referred to as "time-out," which can both mean a time-out of the situation for the participant as well as the inflictor. In any case, he went into time-out, where he thought it was a brilliant idea to sneak an unsavory device called a "whoopee cushion" into his pocket. For those of you who haven't heard of this supposedly entertaining little gadget, it is simply a rubber balloonish contraption that you blow air into. Once full, you then can squish it with your hands or place it under a pillow for an unsuspecting victim to sit upon. Once pressure is applied, it farts. As I've said, unsavory and quite annoying when done repeatedly.

Back on topic, he attempted to sneak it into his pocket. I caught him and told him to put it back, then went about my business. Upon my return, I did not notice that the cheeky little devil had secreted it away once again without my knowledge. I sent him to school with the most disruptive device that could have possibly have gone with him. I notified his teacher, but I fear the damage may already be done.

I came home from dropping the oldest native off feeling quite accomplished and as if I had completed a job well done, only to discover two missing items: the dreaded whoopee cushion and my coffee mug. I looked everywhere for my beloved coffee and remembered that I had placed it on my truck while I was securing the children in their seats. Dearly departed coffee mug, I apologize for my lack of attention to you. Your skid marks left on the bed of my truck were damning evidence of your departure. You will be missed.

And to conclude my tale today, I finish with the tiny natives. Once home, crying and screams filled the household. I assumed they were ravenous and placated them with crackers as long as I could. The tiny male native was satisfactorily compliant. The female, however, would have none of it. In the end, a banana kept her cries to a minimum until the eggs and biscuits could be presented. Once these two delectable golden offerings were given, a strange silence filled our little hut. What a peaceful moment. Unfortunately, it was short-lived, as they soon grew tired of my offerings and wanted to get out of their confinement known as "high chairs" to proceed in the destruction of our hovel. Now, my tale has been told and my breakfast grows cold.

Until next time,
Mom

P.S. The tiny male native seems to think eggs are some kind of insulation. He proceeded to put handfuls of eggs down his shirt. Considering the fact that his shirt clasps together between his legs, this resulted in an eggy bulge at his middle. This habit of stuffing his shirt with random items must cease! I am unsure of how to break him of this.

Week 17

The gloomy weather, the time change, or the change of transport in the mornings. One of these, I suspect, is the culprit. I'm afraid the oldest native has gone off the deep end. Not listening, spitting at students, refusing to follow instruction, tearing up his shoe, sneaking things into and out of school, and the list goes on. I am unsure of the exact cause of this break in sanity, but it is clearly unacceptable!

In other news, the tiny natives are increasingly verbal in very adorable and at times aggravating ways. I fear that the dreaded potty training is approaching at breakneck speed. As I am typing this, the littlest native is patting her waste disposal we refer to as a diaper and all but screaming "Eyepa!" (Which translates to diaper in their tiny native tongue.) These marvelous and yet nasty contraptions allow us to continue our day free of any worry due to bodily functions and the inability to predict the moments of release. However, they are distressingly expensive, to say the least, and rather disgusting. The fact that she notifies me the moment she has relieved herself of her fluid or solid waste tells me that the time for further training is approaching. The middle native has shown no sign of showing these same symptoms, but rather copies his partner in crime and mimics the motions and sounds that she makes. Monkey see, monkey do.

So, this week, I am faced with two realities:

One, the oldest native is indeed getting older, and as a result, he is finding his proper place in civilization. Therefore, he must push boundaries. Unfortunate but normal in this process of education.

Two, the tiny natives (not so tiny anymore) are rapidly changing and growing into little people. This is both a cause of distress and great pride for me as their charge.

In any case, my sanity is once again reaching its limits, but at the same time, my heart is bursting with love. I am finding that despite the hardship this path I have embarked on gives me, I have yet to completely lose my mind. This conundrum has no clear answer, except that it is by the grace of God that we all come out unscathed every day. I pray that He continues His guardianship through these endless weeks and continues to show me the pleasures in this way of life.

Oh dear, I'm afraid I have babbled quite enough for today and clearly my thoughts have run amuck, so I bid you farewell, my friend. Until next time.

—Mom

Week 18

There comes a time in the year when all time devices move ahead or behind one hour. This unfortunate time, it has moved ahead. For the majority of the population, this means an increase in sleep and overall good health. For my tiny village, however, it has unleashed a war. Therefore, I wish an all-consuming fire to engulf the person who invented this ridiculous ritual.

The oldest native now rises at 5:30 a.m. Becoming a part of civilization, he has been introduced to school and has been attending regularly. Regardless of the designated nap time at the said school, he has been refusing to comply and forgoes his nap each day. I still put him to bed at 7:30, which has changed to 7:00, and may rapidly become 6:50 due to his consistent and unwavering pursuit to kill my sanity and possibly the other natives.

His increased attempts to push the boundaries I have set up is rather distressing. From urinating on the floor to repeatedly disobeying, he is beyond trying my patience, for I fear my patience has long since fled the premises. My only hope of preservation is called "time-out." Although this favored term is normally defined as the individual in trouble receiving time away from entertaining activities, it has turned into time for me to flee and gather what little wits I have left to batter against the next attack. I must regroup and discover a new tactic, as this one seems to no longer have a long-lasting effect.

I feel akin to a warrior on the battlefield, hoping the few shots they can get off will make a difference and peace will flood the village once again.

The other two tiny natives are breaking in yet more teeth (does it ever END?) and their battle cries ring out throughout the morning and into the afternoon.

My patience has fled, my resolve is waning, and my heart is heavy with the need to end this battle. I am praying that peace once again fills my small village. That small glimmer of hope is what allows me to hang on. I do not know when I will write again, for surely my end is nigh . . . he will triumph over me and the village will be overrun! Civilization will no longer be the goal and ultimate chaos will reign!

Perhaps if I send a message in a bottle into the sea, someone will hear my plea for mercy. One can hope.

Until next time.
Mom

Week 19

Well, ladies and gents, I made it. The storm seems to have passed and the oldest native has kindly removed his war paint. I am still unsure of what caused this natural disaster of fits and outright rebellion, but I am relieved and grateful that it is over, to say the least.

I commenced folding our clothing today, which is always a bit of a struggle, especially when the adult native is sleeping. Nonetheless, I achieved my goal and provided endless entertainment for the tiny natives with boxes and baskets. Overall, everything is calm once again in my small village and I am left utterly exhausted.

Calm but not quite clean. Due to exhaustion and repeated cleanings, my household is currently in a state of disarray. The tiny natives seem to think it is imperative that the floor be filled with stuffed animals and shoes, as they will not leave them in the compartments I have assigned each. *C'est la vie.* I am actively attempting to train all the natives to clean up after themselves.

It appears a ridiculous song designated *The Clean Up Song* seems to have some effect on their little minds.

On a side note, the tiny natives seem to think that the feline companions are pillows, plush toys, or beds. Their ever-increasing pokes, prods, and squishes are clearly agitating the felines . . . with good reason! I must find a way to break them of this as they are none too gentle with our constant companions. Well, I must bid you adieu as the little heathens are hungry for snack and I dare not keep them waiting.

Until next time,
Mom

Week 21

Whoever is reading this, the hostage negotiations have finally ended. My absence last week was due to a complexity in our village. The adult male native was forced to increase the amount of manual labor required of him. The higher powers that be in his facility decided that a 3 p.m. to 3 a.m. shift was mandatory, resulting in me being taken as hostage by the natives as we only have one operational means of transport in and out of the village. This change in hours lasted a full six days straight, bringing hell on earth for both the adult native as well as myself.

You see, with such long and odd hours, he was unable to contribute to our little village as a result of exhaustion. The natives sensed my weakness and struck. I was confined to a walking distance radius and the little cot we live in with three savages, and no way to relieve their rambunctious energy outside due to weather and/or restrictions. I tried inviting a native from another village over to help expunge my natives' energy, but alas, it only made things worse. Hours of screaming, fighting, and crying afterward, it was a nightmare.

After many, many negotiations with the oldest native, failed attempts at control, the near loss of my mind, and yes, a few tears on my part and BUCKETS on the natives, it is over.

We. Have. Survived.

I have to admit, it was a near thing. Cut off from all outside assistance, my mind was going. Even now, I shudder to think of it.

Well, it is a new week and a new day. So far, the natives have completely transformed into angels overnight! This strange phenomenon is most welcome and I will not question it or try to understand. I am simply basking in the peaceful playing, actually eating, obeying direct orders, and sleeping natives for however long this respite lasts. I pray it lasts a long, long time. I am unsure if I will survive another attack, and if I do, the natives surely will not come out unscathed.

Until that day, my war paint is being shelved and I'm thanking God that we all made it out alive.

—Mom

Week 22

Greetings. We have had another rough week in the village. An awful thing called "the flu" has caused a series of rather unfortunate events. However, I do bring good tidings in the midst of chaos! It appears the last remaining baby teeth are making an appearance in the tiny natives! These small teeth bring me great joy as they will be the last occurrences of fever, fussiness, and all-out fits due to the coming of teeth. Realistically speaking, I will continue to face these trials on a weekly if not daily basis, but I take comfort in knowing that one of the many triggers for them will be disabled.

In other news, the oldest native has discovered the lovely talent of producing burps on command.

This is most annoying.

I must find a way to encourage him to cease "fire" and enforce the rules of manners in the proper places. Essentially, I need to separate play from everything else. I realize I cannot ask this small bundle of energy to give up all forms of play that is not quiet and refined, but I can make the simple request of limiting the amount of rambunctious, and frankly gross, play to the playground or outdoor activities.

Also, Christmas is quickly approaching. This is distressing as well as exciting! It will be the tiny natives' first time opening presents and I am looking forward to the time with family.

Well, I must go tend to my seemingly endless pile of laundry.

Until next time.

Mom

Week 24

Greetings. Last week was a week of holidays, as I was neck-deep in toys, native rivalry, wrapping paper, buildup of neglected chores, and a mad dash to finish all the presents I so foolishly started late. I was absent for week twenty-three; however, you can glean from the description above that it was our usual chaos with a Christmas flavor.

The two youngest natives are fast approaching their two-year mark, which is famously known as the terrible twos . . . rightly so. Suddenly, our village is filled with cries of "MINE," "NO," "STOP," as well as a lot of unintelligible babble and squabbling. While their vocabulary has drastically increased, they haven't quite achieved the status of intellectual arguments as of yet. This results in pushing, stealing, screaming, hairpulling, hitting, and the like.

Most distressing.

The oldest native seems to relish in the new turmoil and has determined that it is his job, nay, his DUTY to become personally involved, referee, or start an argument for entertainment's sake. His most common lines are "But I'm not doing anything!" or "He/she thinks I hit/pushed him/her, but I really didn't"—blatant and irrefutable lies that he somehow thinks will pull the wool over my eyes.

Despite these new and unfortunate events, my peace of mind remains, surprisingly, intact. I do become angry; however, it is more frustration than actual anger and quickly quelled with a time-out for either the natives or myself.

In the midst of this chaos, I have managed to create a better functioning toy system, a proper chores regime, and more quality time with the natives. I am grateful for this much-needed breakthrough in progress, as our village was in sad conditions.

In other news, the oldest native has returned to the educational system of school. This has thrown yet another wrench in our works as he refuses to rest at their facility, causing a more fussy and argumentative native to return. Not only has he ceased listening and following rules in the hovel but at the school as well! I can only hope that time and routine will amend this nasty turn in behavior . . . until the next "holiday," that is.

I used to relish those. Delightful little breaks from labor with relaxation and rest as my only companions . . . they have now become a source of dread. Not because I have all the natives under one roof, but rather that the break in routine causes such an upheaval of authority and structure. By the time I have a new routine and plan set in place and it has become effective, the holiday is over and the intricate map of our day is thrown into the air, to be scattered into the winds.

But I digress. Ultimately, life in the village is always difficult, but little rays of light and flashes of silver linings are always in sight. Until the next shimmer, I bid you adieu.

—Mom

Week 26

My dear Diary,

Where do I begin?

The tiny natives, as I mentioned in my last entry, are approaching what is called "the terrible twos." I have determined that this age should really be called "Wants something but cannot communicate it, so a complete and utter meltdown is required until the said desire is fulfilled."

My head has become a cacophony of screaming, crying, and wailing. My ears are left ringing in the brief moments of silence and my brain has become a graveyard of feelings. I apologize for the dramatics, but I do not understand the logic in screaming for forty minutes due to a blue cup instead of the desired pink one or continuous wailing when the simple word "outside" would suffice.

This skewed logic has my patience wearing thin and my sanity on the brink of destruction, again. To quote the great Dr. Seuss: "And that is not all! Oh no, that is not all."

The oldest native has decided that now is the proper time to completely rebel and question authority. He is acting as an adolescent in his teen years, with his complaining, groaning, and eye rolls . . . rather than the child of four years that he truly is! It gets better.

After acting beyond his years in less-than-satisfactory ways, he regresses into a near-infant state by whining "I caaaaaan't" or "I don't know hoooooooooooow," following and intertwined with crying and throwing himself on the floor thrashing about. Now. The tasks I am asking are quite simple.

"Get dressed." This is a practice we put to use every morning of every day, and he more than knows how to do it on his own. I do not understand how it has suddenly become extremely difficult.

Yet another war. Yet another exhausting day. And I missed yet another week in my entries. Well, I'm putting on my big girl drawers, putting on my war paint, and hardening my resolve. I have a clan to raise and it will not break me.

Now, I do not know when I shall return. If I should disappear, I would only guess that the natives have won and I am tied up somewhere awaiting savage trials. Do not weep for me. This is my job. The wages are nonexistent, the help is miniscule (quite literally), and the mission seems near impossible. But I will go down swinging . . . mark my words.

If there is a next time.
Mom

Week 28

All semblance of sanity and civilized manners have fled the premises.

The screaming won't stop and I cannot think of anything but a quote from *The Lord of the Rings*.

"The ground shakes . . . Drums. Drums in the deep. We cannot get out. A Shadow moves in the dark . . . We cannot get out."

If I survive another week . . . .
Mom

Week 29

After what seemed to be a never-ending week, the natives have decided to give me a bit of reprieve from the crying and screaming. My sanity is returning day by day; however, I do not think a full recovery is in view. My mission is to serve in this foreign land until either they are fully civilized (which, let's face it, may NEVER happen) or I am institutionalized for a mental break. This mission is slowly changing into a semblance of a sentence!

Whining aside:
As I am writing, the tiny natives are having a row over their cup of water. I simply do not understand the issue as once one is finished, the other can then drink. Small arguments throughout the day seem to be helping in developmental progress, but to a civilized adult's view, they are tedious and make little sense. I can only hope that my cries of "share" are heard and absorbed at some point in time. Preferably soon!
I'm increasingly grateful for the moments of silence and peace in my little village. It seems as if I am only allowed to sit down for a few seconds at a time until my break called "nap time" is in effect.

The middle native has begun to shove his hands into his diaper, crying, "Poop!" Then, realizing his rather disgusting mistake, proceeds to cry about the said poop on his hand. It did not take one time to learn his lesson as he is doing it yet again, and I must make a hasty retreat before fecal matter is smeared all over myself and other surrounding objects.

Until next time,
Mom

Week 27

I have sat here quite a while with my fingers hovering over my communication device and I am struggling to describe how difficult the past two weeks have been. The only way I can articulate it is to say that it was an all-out war amongst the natives and me.

While it is not perfect bliss this week, there is a significant drop in screaming. With the terrible twos well underway and the oldest native provoking the already stressful process, it has been a challenge to say the least.

The language barrier, I admit, is breaking down somewhat rapidly. The tiny natives no longer look like babies but mini adults. My heart hurts to think of them in this way as I always refer to them as "the babies" to other adults from different villages. I will not change my label for them just yet.

Being a foreigner is incredibly difficult at times and I question whether I am doing my duty in the correct way. Am I asking too much of them? Am I being too harsh? Is all this just in my head? But then something happens and my heart melts.

The oldest native is headed out the door with a trusted and loved family member known as "grandma," when suddenly, he spins around and says, "Oh! I almost forgot!" Then he wraps his little arms around my neck in a hug. Not to be left out, the middle native throws up his tiny arms and yells, "HUG!" Rather than rolling his eyes or ignoring his mini me, he immediately turns around and gives him a hug. Of course, the littlest native wants one too, so she receives one as well.

Such moments are immensely precious and make all the hardships and frustration worth it. I do believe that I get at least a few things right here and there.

Well, until next time.
Mom

Week 30

Today was very interesting, as I welcomed a native from another village. I was honestly terrified of this entirely possible catastrophe, but it actually went well. We had a few minor hiccups: the middle native not wanting to share toys and the littlest native wanting a toy the foreign native had, so a few rules had to be laid down. And while we all kind of stumbled through the day, it was actually quite lovely.

The oldest native was more polite, shockingly, and very excited about the newcomer. I still have some reservations about the rest of the week, but I have an appointment later this week that should quell or solve the remaining fears I have.

I admit, my world has completely turned topsy-turvy since I have landed on this unfamiliar soil. The past month or so has been particularly grueling; it had me questioning my sanity and the very basis of all my beliefs. A small personal rain cloud had filled my vision and I was unable to see any ray of hope or sunshine. **Obviously, this village has blossomed the dramatic side of me.** But, however mind-bending and difficult this new journey has been, I do see the ultimate good in all of it. My little natives drive me to the very edge of my sanity, but they also melt my heart in such a fashion that it will never wholly be mine again.

Yes, the spills, uh-ohs, unfortunate poopy accidents (others SAY will be laughable in the future, though I highly disagree in the moment), the dirty clothes/dishes/hands, but also the handcrafted gifts, the surprises, the laughter, the dancing, the photos, the songs, and the joy. My little natives are becoming little people, and I am turning into a bit of a native. I constantly worry over education and if I am doing a proper job or using the correct terminology/practices, but at the end of the day, all that truly matters is their happiness and safety. I manage to succeed in at least one of those categories daily, so I will call my mission a success . . . so far.

After all, the only things left to go through are potty training, school, adolescence, accepting my youthful looks fleeing to the four corners of the earth, and the marriage and making of more tiny natives. What could POSSIBLY go wrong?

Until next time,
Mom

Week 30 and . . . a Half

The village is in a constant state of disarray. Playthings scattered to the four corners of the living room, cars underfoot, laundry piling sky-high, and filthy dishes becoming permanent residences in the sink. It appears that the tiny natives love this chaos and dirty surroundings.

This is the only conclusion I can settle on. My reasoning?
Every time I'm in the kitchen trying to clean, they are in the living room reaping havoc. When I am in the living room attempting to pick up, there are either cries of "DIAPER," "MILK," "FOOD," and "WAHHHHHHHHHH," or they are otherwise engaged in destroying the laundry I so carefully folded and put in their room.

Thus, I have concluded that the natives are determined to live in filth and drive me insane.

—Mom

51

Week 32

It has been two weeks since I last wrote. I feel as if a fresh breeze has finally blown into our little village. The prior two weeks have been rough, to say the least. Between the fits, bumps, and the bruises, I had a scrap of sanity left. The adult native has pitched in magnificently and just in the nick of time! I have been relieved from my duties for up to two hours a day the past week to go sweat out frustration and laziness.

Due to my new activity, I have noticed more energy and more willingness to participate in native games, whereas before, I would rather sit and watch. I look forward to seeing this progress and develop into something beautiful!

Presently, the middle native has decided that it was his mission to throw a fit over every minute detail of our lives. He is touched—fit. He sees a toy—fit. He wants water—fit (no asking, just outright fit) This. Is. Bothersome.

I cannot complete my duties as the village caretaker and maintain sanity. As a result, the chores have been grossly neglected.

Week before last, the youngest native was extremely irritable and unsatisfied with everything and everyone involved in her day-to-day. Last week, she has, once again, completely transformed into the little treasure that she is. She is always calm and happy, as well as stubborn and deaf to my requests of assistance, but she is happy whilst she does so. This makes it bearable!

The oldest native has spontaneously combusted into fits of hyperactive activity. I have heard the term "bouncing off the walls"; however, I didn't realize how literal this can actually be. From bouncing around on the leisure cushions commonly known as "sofas" to hopping off chairs, running in circles, randomly screaming unintelligible nonsense in a high ear-shattering frequency, and finally pushing or bumping into the younger natives if not ripping toys from their hands.

Now that you are caught up on past events, my current dilemma is an awful occurrence known as "spring break." Sounds lovely, doesn't it? Anything with "break" in it always has me ready to say yes . . . but no . . . no. Apparently, this break is code for "no school" for an entire week. I adore my charges and would give my life for them! But as well as this so-called break, the forecast has proclaimed that it will rain. Not one day, but, of course, the entire week.

This has me distressed, as my main outlet for native energy is the great outdoors! I can only hope that the days are very warm, so they can play and dance in the puddles as I did when I was an uncivilized native.

So I apologize for the delay and subsequently long letter for this week. I can only pray that I can maintain my schedule next week. After all, I hear that consistency and a regular schedule are imperative to civilizing natives in the wild. Oh, how I long for the days of sleeping in, long showers, and uninterrupted day-to-day tasks.

But I cherish every smile, every happy sound, every dance, and every hug. I am taking it day by day and finding little treasures in each one. Well. Wish me luck, and send a prayer to heaven for me this next week. I have a feeling it will be quite a ride.

—Mom

Week 34

Once again, it has been two weeks since my last entry. What was once a weekly occurrence has changed to biweekly. I apologize for this unexpected change!

To the topic at hand:
The repetitive nature of cleaning, that is almost the very definition of a missionary in my field, has taken a rather violent turn. Whilst I diligently clean one area of our village, the tiny natives are systematically destroying another. Either that or they are in constant complaint of wants, needs, and sometimes even the very fact that I am cleaning.

This is both troubling and aggravating! I have yet to discover a magic trick to alleviate their destructive nature and quell their need to spill . . . everything . . . everywhere.

From crackers to water, our poor carpeted floors are in much need of a washing. However, one cannot simply pull it up and put it in a machine. This causes a great dilemma in the execution of such a large task.

On another note, I am happy to report that the tiny natives have exploded in their vocabulary skills! This causes a more efficient use of communication and creates understanding. I'm also proud that the oldest native has excelled in the art of reading! I have purchased a bundle of books in my excitement and hope he enjoys reading them to me as much as I enjoy listening to him.

While the tiny natives are indeed making use of their vocal demands, it can be quite bothersome. The middle native voices his words in such a repetitive manner that I often repeat it back in a louder voice with a YES attached: "Smiles smiles smiles smiles smiles smiles smiles smiles" and "YES SMILES."

This new form of communication, however useful, can be annoying. I must restrain the urge to interrupt and raise my voice. Practicing patience is a valued tool in this field . . . or so I hear.

This is where I must bid you goodbye. The tiny natives have discovered my stash of Sunday school papers and are currently leaving a torn-up trail across the room of living.

Until next time,
Mom

Week 37 AKA Forever

It has been three weeks since my last entry . . . and . . . .

It has been nine months and one week since I started this journey. I must say . . . going into this mission, I knew my experience would not be rainbows and butterflies as other missionaries appear to experience. However, I did not expect the mental and emotional strain this change would activate. I love my charges more than life itself and it is not only the challenges of caring for them that present the unexpected misery.

The lack of contributing financially to the village has put more of a strain on me than I anticipated.

I am struggling to convey my exact feelings as they are rather jumbled. Whatever my feelings . . . I have decided that it is time to venture out. I am simply unable to carry on and I feel that the tiny natives would benefit more in a trusted educational facility for part of the day. I am not equipped to teach. I feel ridiculous stating this, but it is the truth. I have reached my limit.

Yes. I feel shame and some guilt in admitting this. To put it simply, not every missionary is the same. I have done the very best I can, but have reached a point to where my care has declined. I apologize for the seriousness of this letter, but I felt it was important to show all aspects of my position. From this point forward, I will be fully committed to locating appropriate native care, a second mode of transportation, and a means of income.

I do not know if this will be my last entry. I do not know where this road is leading. I do not know if it is even possible in the near future. All I know is a change is needed for the ultimate care of the natives, for my mental well-being, and for the village to thrive at full capacity.

These past nine months have been an adventure and, as in all adventures, I was dragged through the muck, but I also experienced much joy. I am happy to have had this time and I look forward to seeing what the future brings.

Your ever faithful servant,
Mom

Week 39

Exhaustion has addled my brain the past week. Chores have been sadly neglected and the natives are going through some kind of spell. I am unsure if it is sickness, the "terrible twos," or just simple native rivalry. Whatever the case may be, I am left drained at the end of each day.

However! My charges have shown a remarkable amount of forgiveness and expressions of love after many of the altercations. A much-needed break from my own childhood missionary was administered a fortnight ago for the celebration of my birth. Although last week was very trying, I was able to be patient and care for my charges to the best of my ability.

Whatever trials we face, I will always feel blessed to have such beautiful and wonderful natives in my care. My goal this week is to improve my sleeping habits, and that will hopefully eliminate some of my frustration and aggravation.

It appears that an official part-time job is inconceivable at the moment, although I have managed to muster up the courage to add two natives from another village for at least the duration of the summer. Transportation will be eliminated from the equation, but between the television and the great outdoors, I'm sure we will be just fine. God has been immeasurably good to us, and I pray that my patience and sanity remain unbroken.

Forever theirs,
Mom

Week . . . I Have No Bloody Idea (42)

Good Morrow Diary,

I realize multiple entries indicate that that week in time was harder than the last. I have since concluded that each progressing week is more and more difficult, causing my first week and other weeks pale in comparison.

I apologize for the timing of my entries, as they are becoming more lax and erratic as the days go by. I am still alive.

To give an update on previous events, we have begun, halted, and resumed the training of the "potty" usage. I have tried multiple methods and all of them were depressingly ineffective. From washing multiple undergarments to scrubbing the carpeted floors, my frustration seems unending. Therefore, I have relinquished the reins of the operation, in its entirety, to the tiny natives themselves. This is proving to be the most effective and least abrasive route.

During this rather filthy business, the oldest native has once again donned his war paint. This time, it has extended to the learning facility that he occupies during the daylight hours. It has not only been many years since I have attended the classes known as prekindergarten (the spelling of which, I confess, always baffles me). I have never experienced the adult aspect of it, which in turn releases a whole new world where I must learn to thrive.

This learning facility is a massive center where a throng of natives from multiple villages all converge together, along with several adult missionaries like me, to attempt a collective learning of social skills and requirements.

This in turn also causes a mesh of different cultures, habits, and behavior. Unfortunately, not all the natives are being taught the same values. So, once again, I am fighting an unseen enemy. I believe this mesh of delightful as well as unsavory habits/behaviors is causing confusion or dissension in the ranks of my tiny village. I often feel ill-equipped and unfit for such a demand, resulting in stress and uncalled-for actions on my part as well as all the natives in my care.

I have devised a new tactic for tackling the unsavory bits while promoting the desirable ones. I can only pray that this is accomplished as peacefully as possible.

Some days, I feel as if my war paint has been permanently tattooed across my face. These days are full of trials, but also of sweet moments. The lovely plucked flowers, the laughter, the singing, the hugs, and of course, the time together. These shining diamonds in the midst of such turmoil are true treasures. They, along with chocolate and coffee, are what keep me fueled and get me up in the morning. Today will never come again and tomorrow is always within sight.

Here's to keeping our eyes on today and looking forward to the future.

Until next time,
Mom

P.S. This rather dreary weather does not help matters in the least. Perhaps I should file a complaint.